I AM ENOUGH

A Mindfulness Activity and Coloring Book to Build Confidence in Your Kids

By Visionary Voyagers

A Letter To The Parents

Dear Parents,

First, I want to express my gratitude for taking a chance on our book and investing in your child's growth and well-being.

Being a parent myself, I know that it is one of the most rewarding, yet challenging roles in life. Raising children to be present, confident, and compassionate can be a struggle, especially in today's fast-paced world. That is why I created this book, to help your child learn important values and develop a sense of self through mindfulness and creative expression.

My goal with this book is to provide children with the tools they need to start to understand and manage their emotions in a positive way. Through fun and engaging activities, children can learn to express themselves creatively while developing important skills like self-esteem, confidence, and compassion. Though this book is created to be read, discovered and explored by your kids, I highly encourage you to partner with us in teaching and implementing the tools they learn in this book (You might also be surprised what you'll discover about your kids along the way).

I believe that these skills will not only benefit your child in the short term, but will also lay the foundation for a more fulfilling life for their future.

I hope that this book will be a valuable resource for your family, and I thank you again for supporting our work. We are confident that your child will enjoy the activities and find them both fun and meaningful. If you have any questions or feedback, please do not hesitate to reach out.

With gratitude,

Jonathan

Visionary Voyagers

PS. As a special thanks for buying this book, I've put together a free pdf guide with the Keys to Raising Confident Children. Use it as a tool to help guide your kids to become more confident and value themselves better. I know us parents can use all the help we can get. So simply scan this QR code on the next page to access it.

Thanks again!

* Your FREE Bonus *

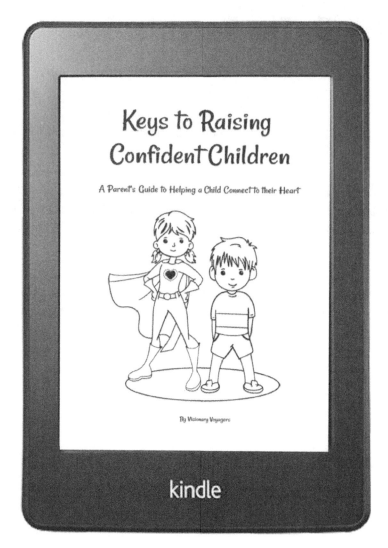

Scan this code to access the PDF

Or go to this link:

https://visionaryvoyagers.com/self-esteem

Also if you like this book, would you mind giving us a review on Amazon?

Your review will help spread the word to other people and help get this resource in the hands of more kids. Thank you so much!

Simply scan the QR code below to review:

Or go to this link:

https://visionaryvoyagers.com/review2

Thank you!

Can I share with you a secret?

My job is to teach kids all over the world just
like you about the superpowers that you already have.

These are 4 symbols. You'll see these symbols all
over this book and they symbolize different types of powers.

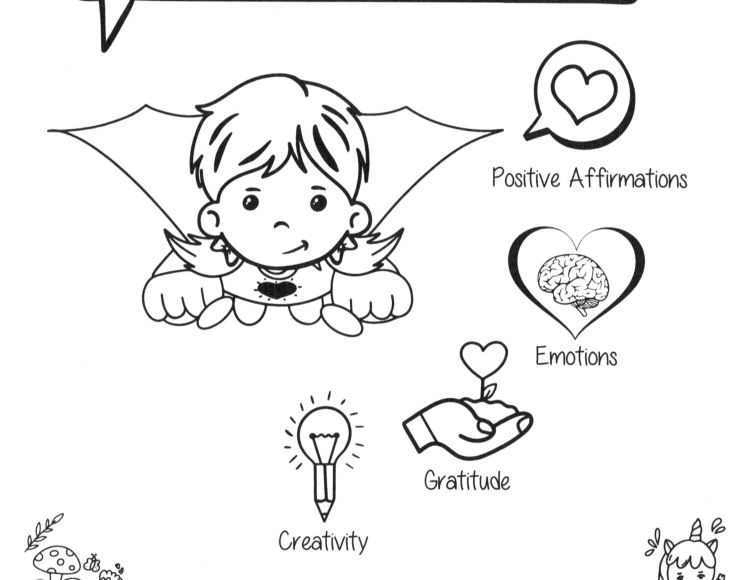

Positive Affirmations

Emotions

Gratitude

Creativity

Most kids don't know that they already have superpowers that they can use everyday to feel better about themselves and see the world in a different way. Come along this journey with me and I'll teach you everything I know.

SUPER TIPS

In the following pages, look for the icon that matches the activity that you want to work on! For example if you're looking for a creative activity just look for the 🖉 icon on the top right hand side of the page.

Most importantly, have fun!

secret superpower

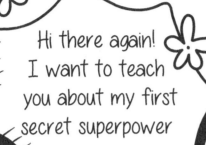

Hi there again! I want to teach you about my first secret superpower

#1

The Power of Affirmation

And what better way to teach you than telling you a story!

Positive Affirmations

That's exactly right! See, our words have the power to change our feelings. It's like having a real super power over our own thoughts!

Can we be superheroes together?

Of course!

Let's practice saying some positive magic words. I call them "Affirmations". Are you ready?

Yes!

Alright, let's say, "I am strong, I am brave, and I am loved!"

I am strong, I am brave, and I am loved!

Excellent! Remember, our words have the power to shape our thoughts and feelings, so let's make sure that the words we say match how we want to feel!

OK, Lev! I want to use my superpower to encourage other kids just like you!

I'm Lev, a superhero of the mind,
With affirmations, I'm one of a kind.
I spread joy and positivity wherever I go,
Helping kids grow, watch their spirits start to glow!

Affirmations, affirmations, they're powerful and true,
They change the way you think and what you say too.
With every word, you'll feel better every day,
So come along with me, let's learn this special way!

Write them down, say them out loud,
Every morning, every night, be proud.
You're amazing, you're smart, you're strong,
With affirmations, your confidence will grow long.

Affirmations, affirmations, they're powerful and true,
They change the way you think and what you say too.
With every word, you'll feel better every day,
So come along with me, let's learn this special way!

I love affirmations so much that I made a poem about it!

Affirmations are like superpowers that can help you become the best version of yourself. Write these magic words out and say them out loud, every day. The more you say them, the more they become true. Let's try it together "I am brave," "I am smart," "I am loved!" If you say it AND believe it, it'll have more power!

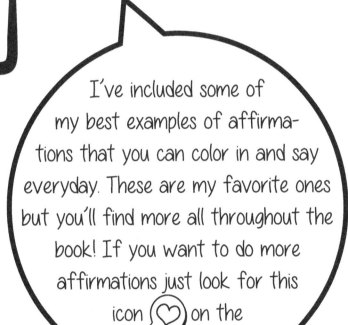

I've included some of my best examples of affirmations that you can color in and say everyday. These are my favorite ones but you'll find more all throughout the book! If you want to do more affirmations just look for this icon 🗨️ on the top right!

Here's a Super Tip

When you start to color these affirmations, also repeat the affirmation in your head. When you're ready, try saying them outloud in front of a mirror at least three times each day. The more you practice, the more power you'll have

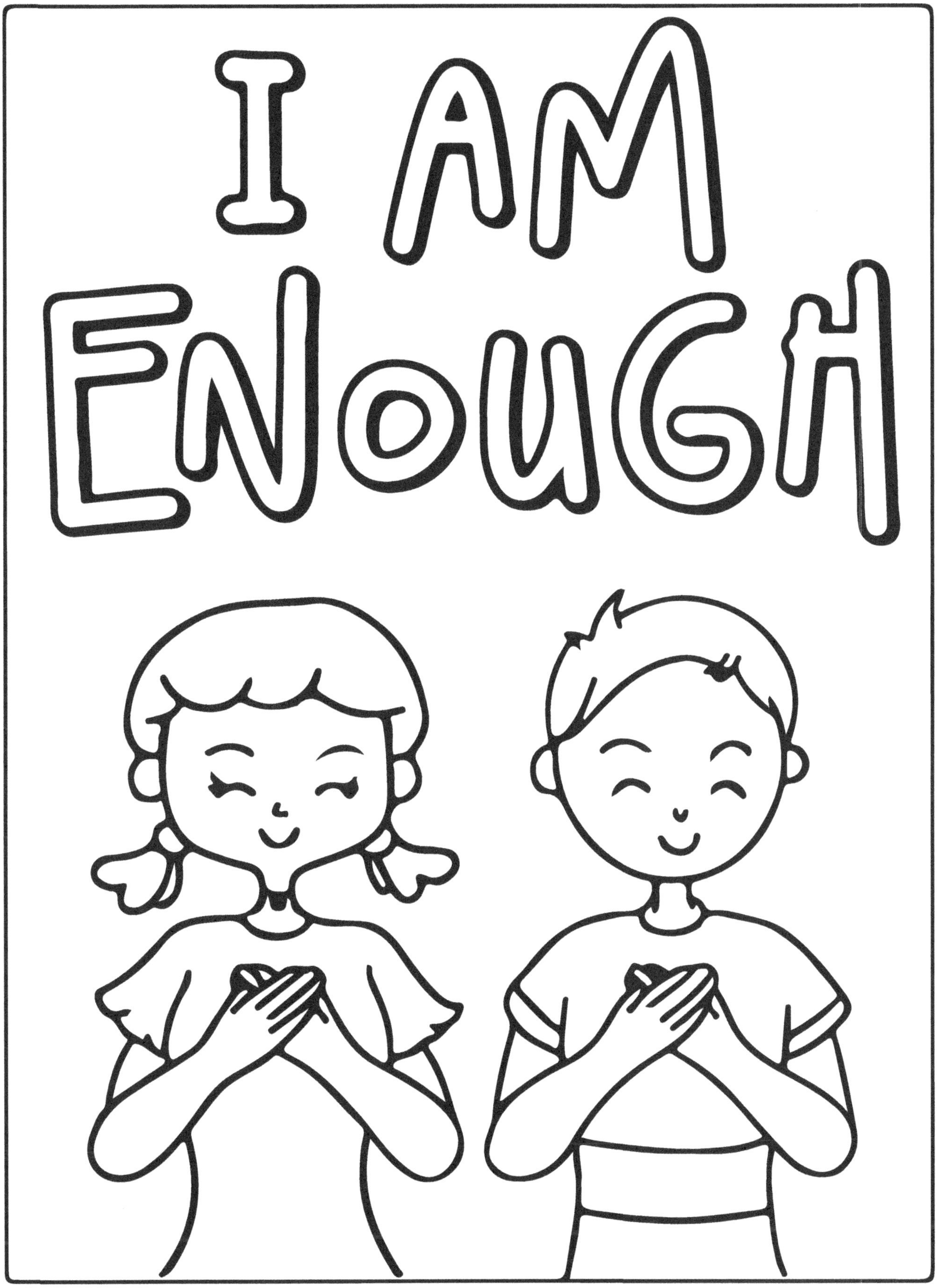
I AM
ENOUGH

secret superpower

Hi there again!
I want to teach
you about my second
secret superpower

#2

The Power of Writing Your Emotions

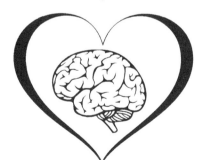

Emotions

Do you ever write down your emotions?

Writing down your emotions is like keeping a diary, but instead of writing about what happened today, you write about how you feel. It's a great way to understand and manage your emotions. Whatever you feel, happy, sad, angry or frustrated, none of those emotions are bad. They are simply a way that your heart navigates the world.

You can use a notebook or a piece of paper and write down how you feel each day. You can use words or draw pictures to express your emotions. It can be happy, sad, angry, or any other feeling. The important thing is to express yourself no matter what you feel.

When you learn to write down your emotions, it can help give you the power to understand yourself better and feel more in control of your feelings. **And that's what makes you a superkid!**

Let's try it out! I've included different worksheets throughout the book to help you write about how you feel. Pick the emotion that you have today and explain how you feel. Draw that emotion and give it a color. Give it a face and show how it feels to you.

Here's a Super Tip

The next time you are feeling sad, frustrated or down, don't hold it in. Use one of the pages we provide and simply draw the emotion you have. Emotions aren't bad or good, they are simply a sign meant to help your body express what it feels.

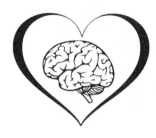

Writing Your Emotions

Color what day it is

Today I Feel:

Write about a time when you felt surprised

SECRET SUPERPOWER

Hi there again! I want to teach you about my third secret superpower

#3

The Power of Gratitude

Gratitude

So you're probably thinking...
"How do I practice that?"

Well, there are many ways to
practice gratitude. You can write
a gratitude journal and write
down things you are thankful for
each day. You can also share with
your family and friends what you
are thankful for at dinner time. Or
you can even say a gratitude
prayer before bed. The important
thing is to focus on the positive and
express gratitude for what you
have.

Today, I'm Thankful for

Color what day it is

S -- M -- T -- W -- T -- F -- S   ___ / ___ / ___

Today I Feel:

What is one thing that you can always count on to make you feel happy?

secret superpower

Hi there again! Today I want to teach you how to unlock our fourth and final super power

#4

The Power of Creativity

Creativity

Do you like to draw? Creativity and drawing are important tools for our emotional well-being. When we draw, we get to use our imagination and express our feelings in a fun and playful way.

And when you look at your drawings, they can bring back happy memories and help you feel positive and good about yourself.

Here's a Super Tip

Don't just limit yourself to drawing. Be creative. Look around you and notice what you have. Everything can be used to create. Scraps around the house, markers, paint, even things in nature can be used to create. Just make sure to get your parent's permission before using these things.

Creativity and drawing are fun and important ways to help us understand and process our emotions.

And that's what makes you a superkid!

Let's try it out!

--->

Draw It

Draw yourself as a superhero or superheroine.

Now that I've revealed all my secrets it's up to you to use them!

It's time for you to take the lead and explore the rest of the book on your own. Remember, this book is all about you and your mindfulness journey.

Look for the icons on the top right corner of each page to choose the type of activity you want to do next.

You're in charge now, so take your time and enjoy the process. And most importantly, have fun with it!

Positive Affirmations

Emotions

Gratitude

Creativity

Writing Your Emotions

Color what day it is

Today I Feel:

Write about a time when you felt silly

Today, I'm Thankful for

Color what day it is

 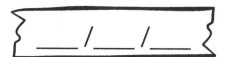

S -- M -- T -- W -- T -- F -- S   ___ / ___ / ___

Today I Feel:

What foods are you most thankful for?

Draw It

Draw the silliest thing you can think of.

I believe in myself.

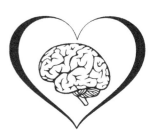

Writing Your Emotions

Color what day it is

 S - - M - - T - - W - - T - - F - - S

 ___ / ___ / ___

Today I Feel:

Write about a time when you felt excited

Today, I'm Thankful for

Color what day it is

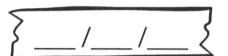

___ / ___ / ___

Today I Feel:

What are you thankful for about your health?

Draw It

Draw a beautiful scene in nature. Use lots of colors!

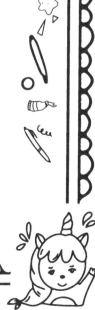

I am Silly

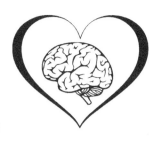

Writing Your Emotions

Color what day it is

___ / ___ / ___

Today I Feel:

Write about a time when you felt discouraged

_____

_____

_____

_____

_____

_____

_____

Today, I'm Thankful for

Color what day it is

S--M--T--W--T--F--S

___ / ___ / ___

Today I Feel:

What are you thankful for about your family?

_____

_____

_____

_____

_____

_____

Draw It

Draw the silliest thing you can think of.

I love to Help others

Writing Your Emotions

Color what day it is

 S -- M -- T -- W -- T -- F -- S

 ___ / ___ / ___

Today I Feel:

Write about a time when you felt sad

Today, I'm Thankful for

Color what day it is

 S -- M -- T -- W -- T -- F -- S

 ___ / ___ / ___

Today I Feel:

What are you thankful for about your mind?

Draw It

Imagine your heart and draw what it would look like. Draw what color it would be and what shape it would have. Does it have a face? Draw it!

I choose to see the best in myself and others

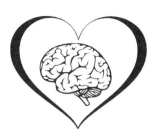

Writing Your Emotions

Color what day it is

 S -- M -- T -- W -- T -- F -- S

 ___ / ___ / ___

Today I Feel:

Write about a time when you felt proud

Today, I'm Thankful for

Color what day it is

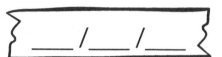

___ / ___ / ___

Today I Feel:

Who is someone you are thankful for today?

Draw It

If these emotions were a picture what would they look like? Draw them! "Joy" "Fear", "Anger", "Sad" and "Surprised"

Writing Your Emotions

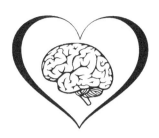

Color what day it is

S -- M -- T -- W -- T -- F -- S

___ / ___ / ___

Today I Feel:

Write about a time when you felt super happy

Today, I'm Thankful for

Color what day it is

S - - M - - T - - W - - T - - F - - S

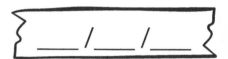

___ / ___ / ___

Today I Feel:

What are you thankful for about your body?

Draw It

Draw what you'd want the world to look like.

I AM COURAGEOUS

Whatever is happening today, IT'S OKAY

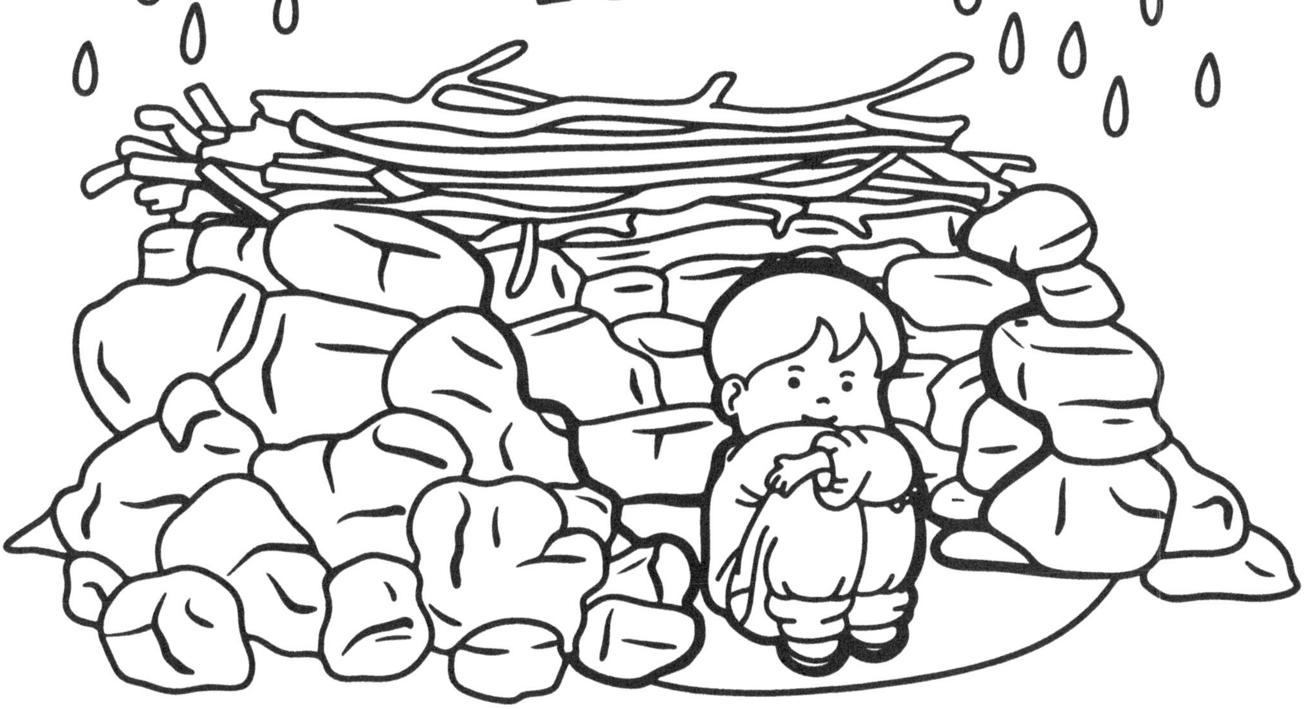

I AM INTELLIGENT

You did it! You now know everything that it takes to become your own superhero too. Though you've finished this book I hope you can still continue to practice everything you have learned.

If you loved the book and it was helpful for you, why don't you tell a friend about it? Also if you spread the word or leave a review, more kids like you will be able to learn about how to be superheroes too!

Tell your parents to use their phone to scan the QR code below

Or go to this link:
https://visionaryvoyagers.com/review2

Lastly, since you're now a superhero it's now your responsibility to share about the powers you've learned with kids just like you.

Your friend,
Lev

Check out our other books:

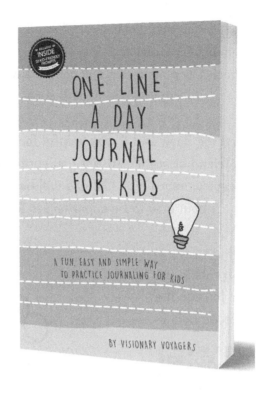

A fun, easy and simple way to practice journaling for kids!

Made in the USA
Las Vegas, NV
12 March 2024